Extreme Sports

Triathlon

by Bill Lund

C A P S T O N E P R E S S

M A N K A T O , M I N N E S O T A

C A P S T O N E   P R E S S
818 North Willow Street • Mankato, MN 56001

Printed in the United States of America.

Library of Congress Cataloging-in-Publication Data
Lund, Bill, 1954-
  Triathlon/by Bill Lund
  p. cm. (Extreme sports)
  Includes bibliographical references and index.
  Summary: Describes the history, equipment, personalities, and
contemporary practice of the triathlon.
  ISBN 1-56065-430-9
  1. Triathlon--Juvenile literature. [1. Triathlon.] I. Title. II. Series.
GV1060.73.L86 1996
796.4'07--dc20

                                        96-9295
                                        CIP
                                        AC

Photo credits
International Stock, cover, Tony Demin, 20; Bob Firth, 17; Langoné, 6; Michael Lichter, 33; Chuck Mason, 14. IronKids, 34, 38. Unicorn/Rod Furgason, 12; Andre Jenny, 36; Aneal Vohra, 4, 11, 28, 41. Greg Vaughn, 8, 19, 22-26, 30, 43.

Table of Contents

Words in **boldface** type in the text are defined
in the Glossary in the back of this book.

Chapter 1
The Triathlon

Some of the world's best athletes are skilled in more than one sport. Basketball superstar Michael Jordan has played professional baseball. Bo Jackson played both football and baseball before he injured his hip. Deion Sanders has played both football and baseball, too. Today is the day of the total athlete.

Many total athletes are triathletes. The word triathlon explains the sport. "Tri" means three. "Athlon" comes from the Greek word for contest. The triathlon is a contest in three different sports.

Triathletes must swim, ride bicycle, and run. Each triathlon includes all three sports. The triathlon is a difficult contest. Triathetes need a wide range of athletic skills.

Triathletes must swim, ride bicycle, and run.

Chapter 2
A Young Sport

People have had swimming and running races for thousands of years. Bicycle races began soon after the modern bicycle was invented in 1876. But putting the three races together is a new idea.

Born in the 1970s

The first triathlon was held in San Diego, California, in 1974. It was organized by a group of runners. These runners wanted to make their training more exciting. They wanted to be more physically fit. They invented the idea of a swim-bike-run race.

The first triathlon was organized by a group of runners.

Many people were interested in biking and swimming. An interest in running was sweeping the world. Many Californians combined all three of these sports. They wanted to become as fit as possible.

Many **skeptics** thought the idea of the triathlon was crazy. They thought no one could be good enough to compete in all three sports. They thought it was too hard on a person's body. They did not think that the triathlon would last long.

The Ironman Triathlon

The triathlon became more and more popular. This was partly because of an event called the Ironman. The first Ironman competition was held in 1978. It had only 15 racers.

Some navy officers in Hawaii were trying to decide which one of them was the best athlete. They held a swim-bike-run competition. The winner was called the ironman. The toughest

The most difficult triathlons are called Ironmans.

triathlons have been called Ironman triathlons ever since.

Both men and women can compete in Ironman competitions. The Ironman is designed for athletes who are incredibly strong. Today, most Ironman competitions draw hundreds of racers.

The Triumph of Julie Moss

One woman's courage helped make the triathlon popular. On February 14, 1982, a triathlete named Julie Moss was competing in the Ironman triathlon in Hawaii. The triathlon was shown on national television.

Moss was in the lead. She was close to the finish line. She could see it. But she collapsed from exhaustion.

That did not stop Moss, though. Other competitors ran past her. She crawled across the finish line.

Moss did not win the competition. But millions of people saw her struggle to finish the race. Moss's determination made more

Both men and women compete in triathlons.

people want to watch triathlons. It made more people want to compete in triathlons.

Moss never gave up. She entered another triathlon in Malibu, California. It was a little more than a year after she had crawled across the finish line in Hawaii. She won the Malibu triathlon.

An International Sport

The triathlon really became popular in 1982. Many people began taking the triathlon seriously as a sport. Prize money was offered in many triathlons. A growing number of people were becoming professional triathletes. Many television networks were broadcasting triathlon competitions.

Few sports have gained popularity as quickly as the triathlon. Triathlons are now held in the United States, Canada, Mexico, South America, Europe, Australia, New Zealand, and Japan. The triathlon has become an international sport.

The triathlon has become popular quickly.

Chapter 3
Kinds of Triathlons

Every triathlon has three common elements. Those elements are swimming, biking, and running. But not every triathlon is the same. Different triathlons are designed for people with different skills and of different ages.

The Sprint

The sprint is the shortest triathlon. In the sprint, competitors swim about one-half mile (about one kilometer). They bike a little more than 12 miles (about 19 kilometers). They

Different triathlons are for people with different skill levels.

usually run a little more than three miles (about 5 kilometers).

The International-Distance Triathlon

The next step up is the international-distance triathlon. This is a much more difficult race. The distances for swimming, biking, and running are at least doubled from the sprint competition.

It takes about as much time to complete the international-distance triathlon as it would take to run a marathon. A marathon is a running race. It takes between two and three hours for top competitors to complete a marathon. The distance for a marathon is just over 26 miles (nearly 42 kilometers).

The Ironman

The Ironman gives triathletes the greatest challenge of all. The Ironman is what most people see when they watch triathlon events on

The running part of an Ironman triathlon is the same distance as a marathon.

television. Seeing Ironman competitions has inspired many people to get into the sport.

Ironman participants swim 2.4 miles (3.8 kilometers). They bike 112 miles (179.2 kilometers). They run 26.2 miles (41.9 kilometers). Few sports are more challenging.

Both men and women compete in Ironman triathlons. Paula Newby-Fraser of South Africa set the record for women in 1992. She completed the Ironman in 8 hours, 55 minutes, and 28 seconds.

The record for men was set by Mark Allen of the United States in 1986. He completed the Ironman in 8 hours, 7 minutes, and 45 seconds. Allen is married to Julie Moss, the woman who crawled across the finish line in the Hawaii triathlon.

Allen saw Moss on television that day. She inspired him to take up the triathlon. Within four years, he held the world record for the triathlon. Within seven years, he had met and married Moss.

Many people get into the sport after seeing triathlons on television.

Chapter 4

Swimming

The swim is the first event in most triathlons. For many triathletes, swimming is also the most difficult event. Most triathletes start as runners or bikers. They add swimming only when they become triathletes.

Picking a Stroke

Triathletes may use any swimming stroke they want to use. Most use the crawl. This is the basic swimming stroke.

The crawl is done face down. They bring their arms over their heads one at time, reaching in front of them. They turn their heads

Triathletes may use any swimming stroke. Most use the crawl.

to the side to breathe. With their feet and legs, they do a flutter kick.

Speeding Through the Water

Triathletes want to get rid of drag. Drag is anything that slows them down in the water. Triathletes make sure their bodies slide through the water easily.

Triathletes wear swimsuits made of nylon or **Lycra**. These suits fit tight. Loose suits would drag and slow them down.

Triathletes' suits must be comfortable. They wear the suit for the biking and running portions of the race, too.

Sometimes the water will be cold. Then the triathlete might wear a wet suit. The wet suit is a long, tight-fitting, rubbery suit. It keeps swimmers warm when the water is cold.

Most triathletes wear a swim cap. This keeps their hair from slowing them down in the water.

Some of the most serious triathletes shave all the hair from their bodies. They even shave their heads. This helps them slide through the water more easily.

Many triathletes wear a swimming cap to reduce drag.

Chapter 5
Biking

Biking is the second part of most triathlons. Triathletes come right out of the water after swimming. They put on their shoes and helmets and get on their bikes. If the weather is warm enough, the triathletes will not even put other clothes over their swimming suits.

Choosing the Right Bike

Triathletes ride lightweight 16-speed bicycles. These bikes are designed for road racing. They are modified so triathletes can get on and off them more easily.

Triathletes ride lightweight bicycles.

Triathletes must be able to sit upright. Regular bike racers crouch over to go faster. Triathletes would get too stiff if they crouched over. If they are stiff, they cannot run well in the next section of the race.

Tools for Triathlon Biking

Many triathletes wear padded gloves. These gloves cushion and protect their hands. Riding a bike without gloves can hurt a triathlete's hands.

Some triathletes wear special cycling shoes. The soles of these shoes are hard and stiff. They are not soft like running shoes.

Stiff soles are better for pedaling. They are more **efficient**. The pedal responds immediately when the triathletes push their feet down.

Reducing Drag

Biking and swimming may seem very different. But in one way they are similar. In both biking and swimming, triathletes can increase their speed by decreasing their drag.

Many triathletes wear gloves when biking.

That is why cyclists stay as close to the bicycle as possible. Then the wind cannot add to their drag.

Triathletes can reduce wind resistance by riding behind another cyclist. The front cyclist works hard to fight the wind. Cyclists following closely behind the front cyclist have no wind to fight against. This is called **drafting**.

Drafting makes the race easy for cyclists who are not in the lead. But drafting is not fair to the cyclist riding in front. In most triathlons, a cyclist cannot draft for more than 15 seconds. After that, the rear cyclist must get out of the draft. Otherwise, he or she will be disqualified.

Triathletes can reduce wind resistance by riding behind other cyclists.

Chapter 6

Running

The running race is the last leg of the triathlon. It is often when the competitors push the hardest. It is their last chance to move forward to win. Running also carries the highest risk of injury.

The Toughest Event

Most triathletes are good runners. Still, running is usually the most demanding part of the triathlon. If triathletes get tired swimming, they can float for a while. If they get tired biking, they can coast. They can rest when they go down a hill.

Running is the most demanding part of a triathlon.

Runners have to carry their whole body weight with every step. Running is usually the last part of the triathlon. The triathletes are already tired from swimming and biking.

Running Shoes

Running shoes are designed specifically for running. They are different than shoes designed for playing tennis. They are different than shoes designed for other **aerobic** exercises.

Runners' bodies are jarred every time they take a step. Running shoes have special padding. The padding protects a runner's legs and back from the jarring. Shoes are a runner's most important piece of equipment.

The Perfect Fit

Triathletes pick a shoe made for their specific weight. A shoe made for a 150-pound (67.5-kilogram) person is different from a shoe made for a 190-pound (85.5-kilogram) person.

Triathletes choose a shoe that fits the shape of their foot. Some people have flat feet. That means that the arches on the bottom of their

Shoes are a runner's most important piece of equipment.

feet flatten out when they step down. They
need a shoe with a high arch built into it. The
high arch protects them against knee or spine
injuries.

Chapter 7

Playing It Safe

B iking, running, and swimming are fairly safe activities. Still, the triathlon is a severe test of an athlete's body. Injuries are always possible if the athletes are not careful.

The Doctor's Exam

Triathletes should see their doctors before they begin serious training. Their doctors will give them several tests. These tests will let the triathletes know if they are ready for a triathlon.

One test is called the maximum-aerobic-capacity test. It tests the maximum amount of oxygen an athlete can use per minute. If an athlete cannot use enough oxygen, he or she is not ready to be a triathlete.

Another test is called the body-fat test. It measures how much of an athlete's body is fat.

Triathletes should see their doctors before they begin serious training.

The Marshalton Triathlon in Marshalton, Pennsylvania, is North America's Oldest and Largest Triathlon.

Exams are important for young triathletes.

Most in-shape athletes have 6 percent to 20 percent body fat. If an athlete's body is too fatty, he or she is not ready to be a triathlete.

Another test is a blood test. This measures an athlete's cholesterol level. If an athlete's cholesterol is not within normal ranges, he or she is not ready to be a triathlete.

Young and Old

A doctor's exam is especially important for athletes over 30 years old. An older athlete needs more preparation than a young athlete. Older athletes' bodies cannot do what they used to be able to do without a lot of training.

Exams are also important for younger athletes who have not been working out. Exams are important if the athlete has a history of heart disease. Exams are important for every triathlete.

Watching Pace

Most triathletes are very competitive. They are driven to win. But the best triathletes know that they must learn to **pace** themselves.

Triathletes who pace themselves do not push their bodies too far. They do not try to make their bodies do things they cannot do.

If triathletes push themselves too far, they might collapse. This means they would lose the race. It also means they could injure themselves seriously or permanently.

Pulse Rate

Triathletes check their **pulse** rate. This helps them keep track of their pace. A pulse rate shows how fast a person's heart is beating.

A pulse rate is checked at pulse points. Pulse points are spots on people's bodies where pumping blood can be felt easily with a person's fingers. Wrists, temples, and necks are good pulse points.

When runners check their heart rates, they count the number of beats they feel in 10 seconds. They multiply that number by 6. If they count 10 pulse beats in 10 seconds, they multiply 10 by 6. Their heart rate is 60.

Maximum Heart Rate

Triathletes also figure out their maximum heart rate. Their maximum heart rate is their age subtracted from 220. If they are 20 years old, they subtract 20 from 220. Their maximum heart rate would be 200.

When they train or compete, triathletes want their heart rate to be between 70 percent and 80 percent of their maximum heart rate. If their heart rate is less than 70 percent, they probably are not training hard enough. If their heart rate

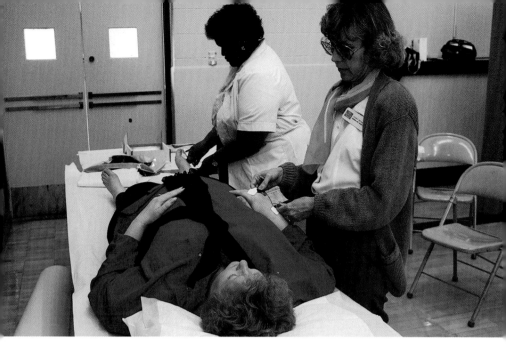

Triathletes learn how to check their own heart rates.

is more than 80 percent, they are probably
pushing too hard.

Preventing Injuries

Triathletes do not want to injure a muscle or
tendon. Such an injury could keep them from
training or competing. It could keep a triathlete
out for weeks or even months.

To prevent these injuries, triathletes warm
up and cool down. Warming up and cooling

down are especially important during training.
They are not as easy to do during competitions.

Warming Up and Cooling Down

When triathletes warm up, they do the same
thing they do during the event. They swim,
bike, or run. Only they do it more slowly. They
swim, bike, or run the first mile at a slower
pace. Then they ease into the faster pace
without risking injury.

Cooling down is done at the end of a swim,
bike, or run. To cool down, triathletes slow
their pace. They do this rather than stopping
suddenly.

When they slow down, their blood keeps
pumping through their bodies at a slightly
faster pace. If they do not cool down after a
hard training session, their muscles might be
very sore the next day.

The Total Sport for the Total Athlete

Triathlons are not the sport for everyone.
Triathlons take a major commitment.

Triathletes are total athletes.

Triathlons require total dedication from the total athlete.

Triathletes must be strong and fast. They need to work hard and carefully. Triathletes must be smart. They need to plan strategies.

It is hard to imagine a more intense sport than the triathlon. It has continued to grow in popularity since it was invented. It will probably be one of the most popular sports of the 21st century.

Glossary

aerobic—exercise that conditions the heart and lungs by making the body use oxygen more efficiently

drafting—driving closely behind another vehicle when racing to take advantage of the reduced air resistance

efficient—to do something with the least amount of effort, expense, or waste

Lycra—a brand of lightweight, stretchy fabric

pace—regulating one's own rate of action, speed, or movement

pulse—regular beats in the arteries caused by the heart pumping

skeptic—a person who doubts things, especially new things

tendon—body tissue that connects muscle to bone

To Learn More

Allen, Mark. *Mark Allen's Total Triathlete.* New York: Contemporary Books, Inc., 1987.

Cook, Jeff. *The Triathletes: A Season in the Lives of Four Women in the Toughest Sport of All.* New York: St. Martin's Press, 1992.

Plant, Mike. *Triathlon Going the Distance.* New York: Contemporary Books, Inc., 1987.

Town, Glenn and Todd Kearney. *Swim, Bike, Run.* Champaign, Ill.: Human Kinetics Publishers, 1994.

Useful Addresses

Bud Light United States Triathlon Series
P.O. Box 1389
Solana Beach, CA 92075

IronKids Triathlons
P.O. Box 1830
St. Louis, MO 63118-0830

New England Triathlon Series
430C Salem Street
Medford, MA 02155

Triathlon Federation/USA
3595 East Fountain Boulevard
Suite F-1
Colorado Springs, CO 80910

Internet Sites

Goodguy's Home Page
http://dove.mtx.net.au/~goodguy

IronKids Olympic Village
http://www.ironkids.com

Ironman Canada
http://web20.mindlink.net/wolf/imc

Triathlete Online
http://www.triathletemag.com

TriChat!
http://www.4-lane.com/sportschat/newsc/
tr_index.htm

Index